SMART BET, BIG WINS

The Complete OddsJam Guide Manual.

By

Paul N Roy

Copyrighted © 2024- Paul N Roy

Disclaimer

The information provided in this book, titled Smart Bet, Big Wins, is intended for general informational purposes only. The content is based on the author's understanding, knowledge, and experience up to the date of publication 16-FEB-2024.

The Author and Publisher make no representations or warranties of any kind, express or implied, about the completeness, accuracy, reliability, suitability, or availability of the information contained in this book. Any reliance you place on the information within this book is strictly at your own risk.

The book is not intended to be a substitute for professional advice, whether legal, financial, or otherwise. Readers are encouraged to seek the advice of qualified professionals for specific guidance related to their individual circumstances.

The Author and Publisher disclaim any liability for any loss or damage, including without limitation, indirect or consequential loss or damage, or any loss or damage whatsoever arising from the use of, or reliance on, the information presented in this book.

While efforts have been made to ensure the accuracy of the information, the dynamic nature of the subject matter may result in changes or updates that are not reflected in this book. The author and publisher do not guarantee that the content is free from errors or omissions.

Any references to third-party products, services, or websites are provided for informational purposes only and do not constitute an endorsement or recommendation. The author and publisher have no control over the content and availability of external websites linked from within this book.

By reading this book, you acknowledge and agree to the terms of this disclaimer. If you do not agree with these terms, please refrain from using this book. The author and publisher reserve the right to make changes to the content, format, or any other aspect of the book at their discretion.

Paul N Roy
16-FEB-2024

Table Of Contents

Introduction
- Purpose and Benefits of Using OddsJam

Getting Started
  - Creating an Account
  - Setting Up Preferences

Core Tools
  - Bet Tracker
  - Fantasy Tool
  - +EV Tool
  - Arbitrage

Free Trial Period
  - Exploring Most Profitable Tools
  - Trial Duration and Features

Individual Tools in Detail
  - Promo Finder
  - Bonus Bet Converter
  - Arbitrage Bets
  - Positive Expected Value (+EV) Bets

Educational Resources
   - Tutorial Videos
   - Free Coaching Sessions

User Testimonials

Frequently Asked Questions
-How Does OddsJam Work?
-What are the Sportsbooks Requirements on OddsJam?
-What Time Commitment is required when using OddsJam?
-What are the Winning Expectations on OddsJam?
-How does OddsJam Address Scam Concerns?
-How can I Balance Effort and Rewards on OddsJam?
-What is the Cancellation Process on OddsJam?

Conclusion
-Customer Support

Introduction

OddsJam is a comprehensive and advanced sports betting platform designed to empower users with data-driven insights, tools, and resources to enhance their sports wagering strategies. The platform stands out in the competitive landscape of sports betting by offering a range of features that cater to both novice and experienced bettors. Here's an overview of what OddsJam is:

1. Odds Comparison and Aggregation.

At its core, OddsJam provides users with a sophisticated odds comparison and aggregation system. The platform collects and compares odds from various sportsbooks, presenting users with a consolidated view of betting opportunities. This enables users to identify the most favorable odds for their preferred events and markets.

2. Positive Expected Value (+EV) Tool.

OddsJam incorporates a powerful +EV Tool, which is a key highlight of the platform. This tool calculates the expected value of bets based on statistical analysis, helping users identify bets with positive expected value. This strategic approach assists users in making more informed and mathematically sound wagering decisions.

3. Arbitrage Betting Opportunities

The platform also facilitates arbitrage betting, a technique where users can capitalize on discrepancies in odds across different sportsbooks. OddsJam's Arbitrage feature identifies opportunities for users to place simultaneous bets on all possible outcomes of an event, ensuring a guaranteed profit.

4. Educational Resources.

OddsJam places a strong emphasis on user education. The platform offers a wealth of educational resources, including tutorial videos and coaching sessions, to help users understand sports betting concepts, utilize platform tools effectively, and implement successful strategies.

5. Community Engagement

OddsJam fosters a sense of community among its users. Through community forums and discussions, bettors can share insights, strategies, and experiences. This collaborative environment contributes to a supportive community where users can learn from one another and stay informed about industry trends.

6. Trial Period and Money-Back Guarantee.

For users who wish to explore the platform's premium features, OddsJam offers a trial period with a money-back guarantee. This allows users to experience the effectiveness of the tools and decide whether it aligns with their betting preferences and goals.

OddsJam goes beyond being a traditional odds comparison site. It serves as a comprehensive toolbox for sports bettors, offering a range of tools, educational resources, and a community-centric approach. Whether users are seeking value in odds, employing arbitrage strategies, or enhancing their overall betting knowledge, OddsJam stands as a versatile and empowering platform in the dynamic world of sports wagering.

Purpose and Benefits of Using OddsJam

In the ever-evolving landscape of sports betting, enthusiasts are constantly in search of tools and platforms that can provide them with a competitive edge. OddsJam emerges as a powerhouse in this domain, offering a purposeful toolkit accompanied by a myriad of benefits that can transform the way individuals approach and experience sports wagering.

At its core, OddsJam is engineered to address the challenges and uncertainties that often accompany sports betting. The platform's purpose revolves around providing users with a strategic advantage, empowering them to make informed decisions, and ultimately, enhancing their chances of success in the complex world of sports wagering.

1.Data-Driven Decision Making: The primary purpose of OddsJam is to shift the paradigm from instinct-based betting to a more calculated and data-driven approach. By leveraging advanced algorithms and analytics, OddsJam equips users with the tools needed to analyze odds, identify opportunities, and make informed bets based on statistical probabilities.

2. Risk Mitigation: Sports betting inherently involves risks, but OddsJam aims to minimize these risks through tools like Arbitrage. The platform assists users in identifying low-risk betting opportunities, allowing them to navigate the market with a more conservative approach and reducing the potential impact of losses.

3.Enhanced Profitability: Ultimately, the central purpose of OddsJam is to enhance the profitability of its users. Through tools like the Positive Expected Value (+EV) Tool, the platform guides users towards bets that have a mathematical edge, increasing the likelihood of sustained success over time.

Benefits of Using OddsJam

1. Strategic Advantage: One of the key benefits of embracing OddsJam is gaining a strategic advantage over other bettors. The platform's tools provide insights and recommendations that go beyond conventional wisdom, giving users an edge in identifying profitable opportunities that may go unnoticed by others.

2.Efficiency in Decision-Making: OddsJam streamlines the decision-making process by presenting users with clear and actionable information. This efficiency is particularly valuable in the fast-paced world of sports betting, where timely decisions can significantly impact the outcome of a wager.

3.Comprehensive Bet Management: The Bet Tracker tool offered by OddsJam enables users to manage their bets comprehensively. From tracking performance and analyzing trends to optimizing strategies, this feature ensures that users have a detailed overview of their betting activities.

4.Educational Resources: OddsJam doesn't just offer tools; it also provides an array of educational resources, including tutorial videos and coaching sessions. This commitment to education ensures that users can continuously enhance their understanding of sports betting strategies and maximize the benefits of the platform.

5. Risk-Controlled Betting: For those seeking a more risk-controlled approach, OddsJam's Arbitrage tool identifies opportunities where users can exploit market inefficiencies, providing a pathway to potentially profitable outcomes with minimized risks.

In essence, the purpose and benefits of using OddsJam revolve around transforming the betting experience from a game of chance to a strategic endeavor. By combining advanced technology, data analysis, and a commitment to user empowerment, OddsJam emerges as a valuable ally for individuals looking to navigate the complexities of sports wagering with confidence and success.

Getting Started

Creating an Account

Creating an account on OddsJam is the initial step towards unlocking a world of strategic betting and maximizing your potential for success in the dynamic realm of sports wagering. This process is designed to be straightforward, ensuring that users can swiftly access the platform's suite of tools and features.

User-Friendly Registration Process

To initiate the journey with OddsJam, prospective users are required to go through a simple and user-friendly registration process. This process is accessible directly from the OddsJam website, providing a seamless entry point for individuals eager to enhance their sports betting experience.

1. Visit the OddsJam Website: Start by navigating to the official OddsJam website. The platform ensures a clean and intuitive interface, allowing users to easily locate the registration section.

2.Click on "Sign Up" or "Register": Look for the prominent "Sign Up" or "Register" button, typically positioned at the top of the homepage. Clicking on this button will redirect you to the registration page.

3.Provide Necessary Information: The registration form typically requires users to input basic information such as their email address, chosen username, and password. Ensure that the provided email address is valid, as it will be used for account verification and communication.

4.Agree to Terms and Conditions: Before finalizing the registration, users are usually prompted to review and agree to the platform's terms and conditions. It's essential to read through these terms to ensure a clear understanding of the user agreement.

5. Complete Verification: Some platforms may require users to verify their email address to activate the account fully. This often involves clicking on a verification link sent to the registered email.

Personalizing Your Account

Once the account is successfully created and verified, users have the opportunity to personalize their OddsJam experience. This may include setting preferences, updating account details, and exploring customization options.

1. Profile Settings: Navigate to the profile or account settings section to customize your user profile. This may include adding a profile picture, updating contact information, and configuring notification preferences.

2. Tool Preferences: Depending on the platform, users might have the option to customize tool preferences based on their specific betting interests. This personalization ensures that users receive relevant insights and recommendations.

3. Security Measures: OddsJam prioritizes the security of user accounts. Users are often encouraged to implement additional security measures, such as two-factor authentication, to enhance the protection of their accounts.

Accessing the Tools

Once the account is set up and personalized, users gain access to the diverse range of tools offered by OddsJam. These tools, including the Bet Tracker, Fantasy Tool, +EV Tool, and Arbitrage, empower users to make informed decisions and optimize their betting strategies.

Creating an account on OddsJam is not merely a procedural step; it's the gateway to a world where data-driven insights and strategic advantages converge. With a user-friendly registration process, personalization options, and a commitment to security, OddsJam ensures that users can seamlessly integrate its powerful tools into their sports betting endeavors, setting the stage for a more strategic and potentially profitable betting journey.

Setting Up Preferences

One of the distinctive features of OddsJam is its commitment to providing a personalized and user-centric experience. Setting up preferences within the platform allows users to customize their interface, receive targeted insights, and align the tools with their unique betting strategies. Let's delve into the key aspects of setting up preferences on OddsJam.

1. Tool Preferences

OddsJam offers a suite of tools catering to different aspects of sports betting. Setting up preferences for these tools ensures that users receive information and insights aligned with their specific interests and goals.

1.Bet Tracker Preferences: Within the Bet Tracker tool, users can customize settings related to how they want to manage and track their bets. This may include options for currency, date format, and other parameters that enhance the usability of the tool.

2. Fantasy Tool Preferences: For users exploring the Fantasy Tool, preferences may involve selecting specific sports or leagues of interest. Customizing player recommendations based on preferred scoring systems and fantasy platforms ensures a more tailored experience.

3. +EV Tool and Arbitrage Preferences: Users engaging with the Positive Expected Value (+EV) Tool and Arbitrage tool can often set preferences related to the types of bets they are interested in. This might

include selecting specific sports, markets, or odds thresholds.

2. Notification Settings

Staying informed about relevant updates is integral to successful sports betting. OddsJam allows users to set up notification preferences, ensuring that they receive timely alerts without being ovoverwhelmed.

1.Alerts for Arbitrage Opportunities: Users keen on exploiting arbitrage opportunities may set up specific alerts to be notified when potential bets with favorable discrepancies arise.

2. Performance Notifications: Bet Tracker users can configure performance notifications, receiving updates on their betting history, win-loss ratios, and other key metrics that contribute to strategic decision-making.

3. Security Measures

Beyond tool and interface preferences, OddsJam prioritizes the security of user accounts. Setting up additional security measures enhances the overall safety of the platform.

1. Two-Factor Authentication (2FA): OddsJam often provides the option to enable two-factor authentication. Users can set up 2FA to add an extra layer of security to their accounts, safeguarding against unauthorized access.

2. Password Management: Users may have the option to update their passwords regularly and choose strong, secure combinations. This is a fundamental aspect of maintaining the integrity of their OddsJam accounts.

4. Language and Regional Preferences

To cater to a diverse user base, OddsJam may offer language and regional preferences. Users can typically set their preferred language for the platform, ensuring that they receive information in a language they are most comfortable with.

Setting up preferences on OddsJam is a pivotal step in tailoring the platform to meet individual needs and preferences. From profile customization to tool preferences and notification settings, OddsJam ensures that users can create an experience that aligns with their unique betting strategies, interests, and security considerations. This commitment to personalization contributes to a more engaging and effective sports betting journey for users leveraging the platform's powerful tools and insights.

Core Tools

Bet Tracker

The Bet Tracker stands as a cornerstone of OddsJam, offering users a comprehensive tool for managing and optimizing their sports betting endeavors. This feature is designed to empower users with valuable insights into their betting patterns, performance metrics, and the overall trajectory of their wagering activities.

Recording and Monitoring Bets

The primary function of the Bet Tracker is to enable users to record and monitor their bets systematically. Users can enter details such as the type of bet, stake, odds, and outcome, creating a centralized database of their betting history.

2. Performance Analytics

The Bet Tracker goes beyond mere data entry, providing users with robust performance analytics. Users can explore key metrics such as win-loss ratios, return on investment (ROI), and other performance indicators. This detailed analysis empowers users to identify successful strategies, areas for improvement, and overall trends in their betting activities.

Trend Analysis and Strategy Refinement

Through trend analysis, users can discern patterns in their betting history. This insight aids in refining strategies, optimizing bet sizes, and adapting approaches based on historical performance. The Bet Tracker serves as a dynamic tool for users to evolve and improve their betting strategies over time.

Bankroll Management

Effective bankroll management is crucial in sports betting, and the Bet Tracker plays a pivotal role in this aspect. By tracking the growth or decline of their bankroll, users can make informed decisions about stake sizes, ensuring responsible and strategic wagering.

Customizable Settings

The Bet Tracker on OddsJam often comes with customizable settings, allowing users to tailor the tool to their specific preferences. This may include options for currency, date format, and other parameters, enhancing the user experience and usability of the tool.

In essence, the Bet Tracker is more than just a record-keeping tool; it's a dynamic instrument for strategic decision-making in sports betting. By providing a centralized hub for bet management, performance analytics, and trend analysis, OddsJam's Bet Tracker empowers users to navigate the complexities of sports wagering with precision and insight.

Fantasy Tool

The Fantasy Tool offered by OddsJam is a game-changing asset for those venturing into the world of fantasy sports. Designed to provide strategic insights and recommendations, this tool empowers users to assemble winning lineups and elevate their fantasy sports experience.

Player Recommendations and Insights

At the heart of the Fantasy Tool are advanced algorithms that analyze player performance, matchups, and other relevant data. The tool offers valuable player recommendations and insights, guiding users in selecting optimal lineups for their fantasy teams. This data-driven approach enhances the probability of success in fantasy competitions.

Customization for Specific Leagues and Sports

One of the strengths of the Fantasy Tool is its adaptability. Users can customize preferences based on specific fantasy leagues, sports, and scoring systems. Whether engaging in football, basketball, baseball, or other sports, the tool tailors its recommendations to align with the intricacies of each fantasy platform.

Real-time Injury Updates and News

Staying informed about player injuries and relevant news is essential for fantasy sports success. The Fantasy Tool provides real-time updates, ensuring that users are aware of any changes that may impact their fantasy lineups. This feature allows for timely adjustments and strategic decision-making.

Maximizing Fantasy Points

The ultimate goal in fantasy sports is to maximize points, and the Fantasy Tool aids users in achieving precisely that. By leveraging data-driven insights, users can make informed decisions on player selections, substitutions, and other strategic moves, increasing their chances of outperforming competitors in fantasy leagues.

User-Friendly Interface

The user interface of the Fantasy Tool is designed to be intuitive and user-friendly. Navigating through player recommendations, matchup analyses, and other features is seamless, allowing both novice and experienced fantasy sports enthusiasts to make the most of the tool's capabilities.

The Fantasy Tool from OddsJam transforms the fantasy sports experience. By combining advanced analytics with user customization and real-time updates, the tool equips users with the tools needed to gain a strategic edge in fantasy competitions. Whether you're a seasoned fantasy sports player or a newcomer looking to enhance your performance, the OddsJam Fantasy Tool stands as a valuable ally in the pursuit of fantasy sports success.

+EV Tool

The Positive Expected Value (+EV) Tool offered by OddsJam is a dynamic and essential resource for sports bettors seeking a mathematical advantage in their wagering strategies. This tool serves as a beacon for identifying bets where the odds are in the bettor's favor, presenting opportunities for sustained profitability.

Identifying Value Bets

At the core of the +EV Tool is the identification of value bets. These are bets where the implied probability of an outcome is lower than the calculated probability, creating a positive expected value. By pinpointing these opportunities, users can make bets that, over the long term, are expected to result in positive returns.

Data-Driven Decision Making

The +EV Tool leverages advanced algorithms and data analytics to evaluate odds across different sportsbooks. This data-driven approach ensures that users are equipped with precise and up-to-date information, allowing for informed decision-making when identifying value bets.

Risk Management

Beyond merely highlighting positive expected value bets, the tool also contributes to effective risk management. Users can assess the potential risks and rewards associated with each bet, enabling a strategic approach to bankroll management and minimizing the impact of potential losses.

Long-Term Profitability

The +EV Tool is not focused on short-term gains but rather on establishing a foundation for long-term profitability. By consistently identifying and capitalizing on value bets, users can build a betting strategy that aligns with the principles of expected value, leading to a more sustainable and successful sports betting experience.

Customization for User Preferences

OddsJam recognizes the diversity of user preferences, and the +EV Tool often comes with customizable settings. Users may have the flexibility to tailor the tool based on specific sports, betting markets, or odds thresholds, ensuring that the tool aligns precisely with their individual strategies and interests.

The +EV Tool from OddsJam is a powerful ally for bettors aiming to go beyond intuition and luck. By providing a systematic approach to identifying positive expected value bets, this tool empowers users with the insights needed to navigate the complexities of sports wagering with a strategic edge, fostering a pathway to long-term profitability.

Arbitrage

Arbitrage, a key feature of OddsJam, serves as a strategic tool for sports bettors seeking to minimize risks and capitalize on market inefficiencies. This innovative tool identifies opportunities where variations in odds across different sportsbooks create a scenario for bettors to secure a profit, regardless of the outcome.

Minimizing Risk

Arbitrage bets, commonly known as "arbs," involve placing wagers on all possible outcomes of an event to guarantee a profit. By leveraging the differences in odds between various sportsbooks, users can create a risk-free scenario where they will receive more in winnings than the total amount wagered, ensuring a positive return.

Real-time Alerts

The Arbitrage tool from OddsJam operates in real-time, scanning multiple sportsbooks for variations in odds that create arbitrage opportunities. Users receive alerts and notifications, allowing them to swiftly capitalize on these opportunities before the market adjusts and the arbitrage window closes.

Diverse Betting Markets

Arbitrage opportunities can arise in various betting markets, including traditional sports, esports, and niche events. The tool covers a wide range of sports and events, offering users flexibility in exploring arbitrage opportunities across diverse betting landscapes.

Automated Calculations

The Arbitrage tool automates complex calculations associated with identifying and executing arbitrage bets. This simplifies the process for users, ensuring accurate calculations of stake sizes to guarantee a profit, and enabling a seamless experience for those exploring arbitrage opportunities.

Enhancing Profitability

Arbitrage, when executed effectively, enhances a bettor's overall profitability by exploiting discrepancies in odds offered by different sportsbooks. While the profit margins per bet may be relatively small, the cumulative effect of consistently identifying and capitalizing on arbitrage opportunities contributes significantly to long-term success.

The Arbitrage tool from OddsJam is a strategic asset for bettors looking to navigate the sports betting landscape with a risk-minimizing approach. By identifying and capitalizing on variations in odds across sportsbooks, users can create a pathway to consistent and positive returns, leveraging market inefficiencies to their advantage.

Free Trial Period

Exploring Most Profitable Tools

The Free Trial Period offered by OddsJam serves as an enticing gateway for bettors to explore and harness the power of its most profitable tools without any financial commitment. This trial period is designed to provide users with a hands-on experience, allowing them to test the effectiveness of OddsJam's tools and witness the potential impact on their betting strategies.

Comprehensive Access to Tools

During the Free Trial Period, users gain unrestricted access to OddsJam's most profitable tools, including the Bet Tracker, Fantasy Tool, +EV Tool, and Arbitrage. This comprehensive access ensures that users can explore the full spectrum of tools that contribute to strategic decision-making and potentially enhance their profitability.

Hands-On Exploration

The trial period encourages users to immerse themselves in the platform, trying out different tools and features to understand how they integrate into their betting strategies. This hands-on exploration allows users to gauge the usability, functionality, and effectiveness of OddsJam's tools within the context of their individual preferences and objectives.

Real-Time Application

Users can apply the tools in real-time to their ongoing betting activities, allowing them to experience the immediate impact on their decision-making process. This real-time application is instrumental in helping users assess the practical benefits of

OddsJam's tools and understand how they align with their unique betting goals.

Risk-Free Evaluation

The Free Trial Period provides a risk-free environment for users to evaluate the profitability and value offered by OddsJam's tools. By experiencing the platform without financial commitment, users can make informed decisions about the potential long-term benefits and relevance of OddsJam to their sports betting journey.

Informed Subscription Decisions

The trial period empowers users to make informed subscription decisions. Having experienced the tools firsthand, users can evaluate whether the platform aligns with their betting strategies, preferences, and overall objectives. This informed decision-making process contributes to a more satisfying and valuable subscription experience.

In essence, the Free Trial Period offered by OddsJam is not merely a brief introduction but a substantial opportunity for users to immerse themselves in the platform's most profitable tools. By exploring, testing, and applying these tools in a risk-free environment, bettors can make informed decisions about incorporating OddsJam into their sports betting toolkit, potentially unlocking a new level of strategic advantage and profitability.

Trial Duration and Features

The Trial Duration and Features provided by OddsJam offer users a strategic window to experience the platform's capabilities and evaluate its effectiveness in enhancing their sports betting endeavors. This trial period is crafted to provide users with a comprehensive understanding of the platform's features and their potential impact on betting strategies.

Generous Trial Period

OddsJam typically provides users with a generous trial period, often spanning seven days. This duration allows ample time for users to explore the platform, test its tools, and gain hands-on experience in leveraging the features to enhance their betting decisions.

Unrestricted Access to Premium Features

During the trial period, users enjoy unrestricted access to premium features. This includes the most profitable tools such as the Bet Tracker, Fantasy Tool, +EV Tool, and Arbitrage. The goal is to provide users with a holistic experience, allowing them to explore the full range of tools that OddsJam offers.

Real-Time Application of Tools

The trial period encourages users to apply the tools in real-time to their ongoing betting activities. This hands-on experience is crucial in understanding how the features integrate into their decision-making process and assessing their practical impact on optimizing betting strategies.

Access to Educational Resources

In addition to the tools, users during the trial period can explore educational resources such as tutorial videos and coaching sessions. These resources provide valuable insights into utilizing OddsJam effectively, ensuring that users can make the most of the platform's features and refine their understanding of strategic betting approaches.

Transparent Overview of Platform Benefits

The trial period serves as a transparent overview of the benefits offered by OddsJam. Users can evaluate the platform's strengths, assess how it aligns with their betting goals, and make informed decisions about its long-term suitability for their sports wagering journey.

The Trial Duration and Features provided by OddsJam aim to deliver a comprehensive and immersive experience. By offering users ample time to explore premium features, apply tools in real-time, and access educational resources, OddsJam ensures that users can make informed decisions about incorporating the platform into their sports betting toolkit. This strategic trial period sets the stage for a potential long-term partnership, where users can leverage OddsJam's features to enhance their betting strategies and pursue sustained success in the dynamic world of sports wagering.

Individual Tools in Detail

Promo Finder

The Promo Finder feature on OddsJam emerges as a valuable tool for sports bettors seeking to optimize their wagering experience by unlocking promotional offers and bonus bets. This feature is designed to scour various sportsbooks to identify and present users with lucrative promotions, enhancing their overall betting value.

Centralized Promo Discovery

Promo Finder acts as a centralized hub for discovering promotional offers across different sportsbooks. Instead of manually searching through numerous platforms, users can rely on Promo Finder to streamline the process, presenting them with a curated list of available promotions.

Diverse Promotional Offers

Promo Finder caters to a diverse range of promotional offers, including bonus bets, free bets, enhanced odds, and other enticing deals provided by sportsbooks. This diversity ensures that users can explore a variety of promotions and choose those that align with their betting preferences and strategies.

Increased Betting Value

By leveraging Promo Finder, users can significantly increase their overall betting value. Identifying and capitalizing on promotional offers provides an additional layer of profitability, allowing users to maximize their returns without increasing their inherent risk.

Time Efficiency

Searching for promotions across multiple sportsbooks can be time-consuming. Promo Finder addresses this challenge by offering a time-efficient solution. Users can access a consolidated list of promotions, saving time and ensuring they never miss out on potentially lucrative offers.

Tailored Recommendations

The Promo Finder feature on OddsJam often comes with customization options, allowing users to tailor their preferences. This might include filtering promotions based on specific sports, events, or types of bonuses, ensuring that users receive recommendations aligned with their betting interests.

Promo Finder is not just a tool for discovering promotions; it's a strategic asset for enhancing the overall betting value. By centralizing promotional offers, providing diverse options, and saving users time, OddsJam's Promo Finder empowers sports bettors to make more informed decisions and capitalize on the myriad opportunities presented by sportsbooks.

Bonus Bet Converter

The Bonus Bet Converter feature on OddsJam is a game-changing tool designed to empower sports bettors by converting promotional bonuses into tangible withdrawals. This innovative feature maximizes the value of bonus bets, providing users with a strategic approach to turn promotional incentives into real profits.

Unlocking Bonus Bet Value

Bonus Bet Converter focuses on unlocking the full value of bonus bets provided by sportsbooks. It goes beyond merely using bonus bets for wagering and introduces a systematic method for converting these promotional incentives into withdrawable funds.

Algorithmic Insights

The feature leverages advanced algorithms to provide users with insights into betting combinations that can optimize the conversion of bonus bets. These algorithms analyze odds, markets, and potential outcomes, guiding users towards strategically placing bets that enhance the likelihood of converting bonuses into real money.

Systematic Approach to Wagering

Bonus Bet Converter introduces a systematic and calculated approach to wagering with bonus funds. Rather than relying on intuition, users can make informed decisions based on data-driven insights, increasing the probability of successful bets and subsequent withdrawal of profits.

Maximizing Profitability

By utilizing the Bonus Bet Converter, users can maximize the profitability of their promotional bonuses. The tool identifies optimal betting combinations, ensuring that users make the most of the bonus bets provided by sportsbooks and potentially generate additional income.

User-Friendly Interface

The Bonus Bet Converter feature is designed with user-friendliness in mind. The interface is intuitive, allowing users to easily navigate through betting combinations, place strategic wagers, and track the progress of their bonus conversion journey.

Bonus Bet Converter transforms the traditional approach to bonus bet utilization. By introducing a systematic and algorithmically-driven method for converting bonus bets into real withdrawals, OddsJam empowers users with a strategic tool that aligns with their ultimate goal of maximizing profitability in the dynamic world of sports betting.

Arbitrage Bets

Arbitrage Bets, a key feature on OddsJam, provides sports bettors with a unique opportunity to capitalize on market inefficiencies and secure profits with minimal risk. This tool identifies and presents users with low-risk betting combinations where variations in odds across different sportsbooks create a scenario for guaranteed returns.

Identifying Low-Risk Opportunities

The core function of the Arbitrage Bets feature is to identify opportunities were the odds offered by various sportsbooks create a situation where a bettor can place wagers on all possible outcomes of an event and still secure a profit. By pinpointing these low-risk opportunities, users can engage in strategic and profitable betting.

Real-Time Alerts and Notifications

Arbitrage Bets operate in real-time, constantly scanning sportsbooks for variations in odds that present arbitrage opportunities. Users receive instant alerts and notifications, ensuring that they can act swiftly before the market adjusts and the opportunity diminishes. This real-time feature is crucial for users seeking to capitalize on timely and lucrative arbitrage scenarios.

Streamlined Betting Combinations

Arbitrage Bets on OddsJam simplify the process of identifying and executing low-risk betting combinations. The tool typically provides users with clear information on the specific bets to place, the amounts to wager, and the potential profit margins. This streamlined approach enhances the user experience and facilitates easy implementation of arbitrage strategies.

Enhancing Profitability

Engaging in arbitrage betting with OddsJam is a strategic approach to enhancing overall profitability. While individual profits per bet may be relatively small, the cumulative effect of consistently identifying and capitalizing on low-risk arbitrage opportunities contributes significantly to long-term success in sports wagering.

Risk Management and Bankroll Growth

Arbitrage Bets inherently involve minimal risk, making them a valuable tool for effective risk management. By systematically capitalizing on these opportunities, users can contribute to the growth of their bankroll while mitigating potential losses associated with traditional betting methods.

Arbitrage Bets on OddsJam empower users with a unique and strategic approach to sports betting. By identifying low-risk opportunities in real-time, streamlining betting combinations, and providing a pathway to consistent profits, this feature stands as a valuable asset for bettors seeking to navigate the sports betting landscape with a calculated and advantageous approach.

Positive Expected Value (+EV) Bets

The Positive Expected Value (+EV) Bets feature on OddsJam is a powerful tool that equips sports bettors with a systematic approach to identifying wagers where the odds are in their favor. This data-driven tool assesses various betting opportunities, highlighting those with a positive expected value and providing users with a strategic advantage in their sports betting endeavors.

Identifying Profitable Opportunities

The +EV Bets feature focuses on identifying bets where the expected value is positive. In essence, these are opportunities where the calculated probability of an outcome's occurrence exceeds the implied probability reflected in the odds provided by sportsbooks. By pinpointing these profitable opportunities, users can make informed betting decisions with a higher likelihood of long-term success.

Algorithmic Analysis

The +EV Bets feature utilizes advanced algorithms and data analytics to analyze odds across different sportsbooks. This algorithmic analysis ensures that users receive accurate and up-to-date information, allowing them to make decisions based on a comprehensive understanding of the betting landscape.

Informed Decision-Making

By leveraging +EV Bets, users can make more informed decisions when selecting their wagers. The tool provides insights into which bets offer a mathematical edge, allowing users to prioritize opportunities that align with their overall betting strategy and long-term profitability goals.

Long-Term Profitability

The +EV Bets feature is not focused on short-term gains but rather on establishing a foundation for long-term profitability. By consistently identifying and capitalizing on opportunities where the odds are undervalued, users can contribute to sustained success and growth in their sports betting endeavors.

Customizable Preferences

OddsJam recognizes the diversity of user preferences, and the +EV Bets feature often comes with customizable settings. Users may have the flexibility to tailor the tool based on specific sports, betting markets, or odds thresholds, ensuring that the tool aligns precisely with their individual strategies and interests.

The Positive Expected Value Bets feature on OddsJam empowers users with a strategic advantage in the dynamic world of sports betting. By providing a systematic approach to identifying profitable opportunities, leveraging algorithmic analysis, and offering customization options, this tool stands as a valuable asset for bettors seeking a data-driven and strategic edge in their wagering activities.

Educational Resources

Tutorial Videos

OddsJam goes beyond being a platform solely for sports betting tools; it is committed to ensuring users have the knowledge and expertise to maximize the potential of these tools. The Educational Resources section, specifically the Tutorial Videos, serves as a valuable repository of insights, strategies, and guidance to assist users in navigating the intricacies of sports betting.

Comprehensive Learning Experience

Tutorial Videos on OddsJam offer a comprehensive learning experience, covering various aspects of sports betting, utilizing platform tools, and implementing strategic approaches. From basic concepts to advanced strategies, these videos cater to users of all levels, providing a structured learning path.

Tool-Specific Guidance

Each tool offered by OddsJam is accompanied by dedicated tutorial videos. Users can delve into these videos to gain a deeper understanding of how to effectively use tools such as Bet Tracker, Fantasy Tool, +EV Tool, Arbitrage, and more. This tool-specific guidance ensures users can make the most of each feature.

Visual Learning

Tutorial Videos leverage the power of visual learning, making complex concepts more accessible. Whether explaining the functionality of a specific tool, demonstrating strategic decision-making, or illustrating betting concepts, these videos enhance understanding through visual aids and examples.

Accessible Anytime, Anywhere

The flexibility of Tutorial Videos allows users to access educational content at their convenience. Whether on a desktop, tablet, or mobile device, users can engage with the tutorial videos anytime, anywhere, making learning a seamless part of their sports betting journey.

Continuous Updates

The educational content is not static; OddsJam ensures that the Tutorial Videos are regularly updated to align with industry trends, new features, and evolving best practices. Users can stay informed about the latest strategies and tools, enhancing their proficiency in the dynamic landscape of sports betting.

Tutorial Videos within OddsJam's Educational Resources contribute significantly to the platform's commitment to user empowerment. By offering a rich source of knowledge, strategy insights, and practical demonstrations, OddsJam ensures that users can enhance their sports betting skills, make informed decisions, and derive maximum value from the platform's robust suite of tools.

Free Coaching Sessions

The inclusion of Free Coaching Sessions in OddsJam's Educational Resources exemplifies the platform's dedication to providing users with personalized guidance and support in their sports betting journey. These sessions offer a unique opportunity for users to engage directly with experienced coaches, receive tailored advice, and refine their betting strategies.

Personalized Guidance

Free Coaching Sessions on OddsJam provide users with a personalized and interactive learning experience. Experienced coaches, well-versed in sports betting dynamics, engage with users on an individual basis, offering insights and guidance tailored to their specific needs and goals.

Strategic Decision-Making

Coaches in these sessions assist users in refining their strategic decision-making process. Whether it's optimizing the use of OddsJam tools, understanding betting markets, or developing effective bankroll management strategies, the coaching sessions contribute to users making more informed and strategic choices.

Platform Familiarization

For users new to the OddsJam platform, coaching sessions serve as a valuable resource for platform familiarization. Coaches guide users through tool functionalities, explain features, and address any queries, ensuring that users can navigate the platform confidently and effectively.

Q&A Interaction

Free Coaching Sessions facilitate a dynamic question-and-answer interaction. Users can seek clarification on specific concepts, discuss challenges they face in their betting approach, and receive real-time responses from coaches. This interactive format enhances the learning experience and ensures that users' queries are directly addressed.

Continuous Learning Opportunities

OddsJam understands that learning is an ongoing process. By offering Free Coaching Sessions, the platform provides users with continuous learning opportunities. Coaches stay abreast of industry trends and updates, ensuring that users receive the most relevant and up-to-date advice in the ever-evolving landscape of sports betting.

Free Coaching Sessions stand as a cornerstone of OddsJam's commitment to user education and empowerment. By providing direct access to experienced coaches, the platform goes beyond tools and features, offering users a personalized learning journey that enhances their sports betting skills, strategy development, and overall success in the dynamic world of sports wagering.

Subscription Plans

Promo Optimizer Plan

The Promo Optimizer Plan on OddsJam is a comprehensive and strategic subscription offering tailored for users looking to maximize the value of promotional offers and bonuses provided by sportsbooks. This plan combines a range of advanced tools to optimize promotional opportunities, ensuring users can leverage bonuses to their fullest potential.

Centralized Promo Optimization

The Promo Optimizer Plan serves as a centralized hub for users to optimize promotional offers effectively. It consolidates tools like Promo Finder, Bonus Bet Converter, and other key features, providing a unified platform to streamline and enhance the overall value derived from promotions.

Bonus Bet Conversion Strategies

At the core of the Promo Optimizer Plan is the Bonus Bet Converter, a feature designed to convert bonus bets into tangible withdrawals. This plan equips users with advanced strategies and algorithms, guiding them on how to strategically utilize these bonus bets across various markets and sports, turning them into real profits.

Low-Hold and Middles Tools

The plan includes tools such as Low-Hold and Middles, designed to further optimize promotional opportunities. Low-Hold aids in identifying low-risk bets, minimizing potential losses, while Middles exploit discrepancies in odds between different sportsbooks, creating opportunities for additional profits.

Mobile App Access

Subscribers to the Promo Optimizer Plan enjoy the convenience of accessing these powerful tools through the OddsJam Mobile App. This ensures flexibility and real-time optimization, allowing users to make strategic decisions on the go and capitalize on promotional offers swiftly.

Unlimited Line Shopping

The plan provides users with unlimited access to Line Shopping, allowing them to compare odds across various sportsbooks easily. This ensures that users can make well-informed decisions, optimizing their betting strategies and capitalizing on the most favorable odds available in the market.

The Promo Optimizer Plan on OddsJam is a strategic subscription package designed for users keen on maximizing the value of promotional offers. By combining advanced tools, algorithms, and features, this plan empowers users to not only discover lucrative promotions but also optimize their utilization, contributing to enhanced profitability in the dynamic landscape of sports betting.

Positive EV Plan

The Positive EV Plan on OddsJam stands as a premium subscription offering that caters to sports bettors aiming for sustained success through a strategic and data-driven approach. This comprehensive plan encompasses a suite of tools and features designed to identify and capitalize on positive expected value (+EV) opportunities, providing users with a systematic advantage in the competitive realm of sports betting.

Unlimited Access to Most Profitable Tools

The Positive EV Plan offers users unrestricted access to OddsJam's most profitable tools. This includes the +EV Tool, Arbitrage, and other key features that empower users to make data-driven decisions, identify value bets, and maximize profitability over the long term.

+EV Tool for Informed Betting

At the core of this plan is the +EV Tool, a sophisticated analytics tool that evaluates odds across different sportsbooks. By identifying bets with positive expected value, users gain a mathematical edge, allowing for strategic and informed betting decisions that align with a long-term profitability strategy.

Arbitrage Opportunities

Subscribers to the Positive EV Plan benefit from the Arbitrage feature, which identifies low-risk bets across multiple sportsbooks. This allows users to capitalize on market inefficiencies, making simultaneous wagers on all possible outcomes of an event to secure guaranteed profits.

Parlay Builder for Enhanced Odds

The plan includes the Parlay Builder feature, enabling users to create and optimize parlays. By strategically combining multiple bets into a single wager, users can enhance their odds and potentially amplify their returns, contributing to an overall more lucrative betting experience.

Exclusive Educational Resources

Beyond tools, the Positive EV Plan provides users with exclusive access to advanced educational resources. This includes in-depth tutorial videos, coaching sessions, and a wealth of content designed to enhance users' understanding of betting strategies, risk management, and the effective utilization of OddsJam's features.

Customizable Settings for Personal Preferences

Recognizing the diversity of user preferences, the Positive EV Plan often comes with customizable settings. Users can tailor the tool to their specific preferences, such as selecting preferred sports, setting odds thresholds, and personalizing parameters, ensuring that the plan aligns precisely with individual strategies and interests.

Real-Time Push Notifications

The Positive EV Plan keeps users in the loop with real-time push notifications. Whether it's an identified +EV opportunity, an arbitrage alert, or updates on promotions, subscribers receive instant notifications, allowing them to stay ahead of the market and capitalize on time-sensitive opportunities.

Auto Refresh and Line Movement History

The plan includes features like Auto Refresh and Line Movement History, enhancing the user experience. Auto Refresh ensures that odds and information are consistently updated in real-time, while Line Movement History provides insights into how odds have shifted over time, aiding users in making more informed decisions.

Circa Vegas Odds for Precision

Subscribers gain access to Circa Vegas Odds, providing precise and accurate odds from one of the renowned sportsbooks. This feature ensures that users have access to reliable data, enhancing the quality of their decision-making process.

The Positive EV Plan on OddsJam is a comprehensive subscription package designed for sports bettors seeking a strategic edge. By combining advanced tools, educational resources, and customization options, this plan equips users with the tools and knowledge needed to navigate the complexities of sports betting with precision and profitability. Subscribers to the Positive EV Plan embark on a journey that goes beyond traditional wagering, leveraging data-driven insights for sustained success in the dynamic world of sports betting.

Platinum Plan

The Platinum Plan on OddsJam stands as the pinnacle of subscription offerings, providing an unparalleled toolbox for full-time bettors who seek the highest level of sophistication and precision in their sports wagering strategies. This comprehensive plan incorporates an array of advanced features and exclusive tools that cater to users aiming for excellence and maximum profitability in the dynamic world of sports betting.

All-Inclusive Access to Premium Features.

The Platinum Plan grants users all-inclusive access to not only the most profitable tools like the +EV Tool, Arbitrage, and Parlay Builder but also introduces exclusive features tailored for advanced betting strategies. This comprehensive access ensures that subscribers can leverage the full spectrum of tools available on the OddsJam platform.

Live Game Odds and Global Sportsbooks

One of the standout features of the Platinum Plan is access to live game odds and a global selection of sportsbooks. Subscribers can make real-time decisions based on the latest odds, ensuring they are at the forefront of the betting market and can capitalize on evolving opportunities as events unfold.

Real-Time Push Notifications and Auto Refresh

The plan keeps users informed with real-time push notifications, alerting them to valuable opportunities, changes in odds, or other time-sensitive information. Auto Refresh ensures that odds and data are consistently updated, allowing users to maintain a competitive edge by staying abreast of the latest developments.

Line Movement History and Circa Vegas Odds

The Platinum Plan includes advanced features such as Line Movement History and Circa Vegas Odds. Line Movement History provides users with insights into how odds have evolved over time, facilitating more informed decision-making. Circa Vegas Odds offer access to precise and reliable odds from a reputable sportsbook, enhancing the accuracy of users' analyses.

Real Time Push Notifications and Auto Refresh

Real-time push notifications are a vital component of the Platinum Plan, ensuring users receive instant alerts about potential opportunities or changes in odds. The Auto Refresh feature guarantees that users have access to the most up-to-date information, allowing for swift and informed decision-making.

Enhanced Platform Experience

Subscribers to the Platinum Plan benefit from an enhanced platform experience, with features designed to optimize usability and efficiency. The user-friendly interface coupled with advanced functionalities ensures a seamless and sophisticated experience for users navigating the complexities of sports betting.

Global Sportsbooks and Mobile App Access

The inclusion of global sportsbooks expands the horizons for users, offering a diverse range of betting options from around the world. Additionally, the accessibility of these features through the OddsJam Mobile App ensures that users can engage with the Platinum Plan's tools and capabilities anytime, anywhere, providing flexibility for those on the move.

Real Time Push Notifications and Auto Refresh

Real-time push notifications are a vital component of the Platinum Plan, ensuring users receive instant alerts about potential opportunities or changes in odds. The Auto Refresh feature guarantees that users have access to the most up-to-date information, allowing for swift and informed decision-making.

The Platinum Plan on OddsJam is a premium subscription offering tailored for those who view sports betting as a serious endeavor. By integrating advanced tools, exclusive features, and real-time capabilities, this plan caters to the needs of professional bettors, providing them with the resources and insights necessary to navigate the intricate landscape of sports wagering with precision and sophistication. Subscribers to the Platinum Plan embark on a journey that transcends traditional betting, gaining access to a comprehensive toolbox designed for excellence and success in the competitive world of sports betting.

Pricing and Savings

Monthly and Annual Billing Options

The Pricing and Savings structure on OddsJam offers users flexibility with both monthly and annual billing options, allowing them to choose a subscription plan that aligns with their preferences and betting strategies. This approach caters to a diverse user base, whether they are looking for a short-term commitment or seeking long-term value and savings.

Monthly Billing

For users who prefer flexibility and a shorter commitment period, the monthly billing option is an ideal choice. This allows subscribers to access the chosen plan on a month-to-month basis, providing the freedom to evaluate the effectiveness of the platform tools and features without a long-term commitment. The monthly billing option is particularly suitable for those who may want to explore OddsJam for a specific period or have varying betting needs.

Annual Billing

The annual billing option offers users significant savings and advantages for a more extended commitment. By opting for an annual subscription, users typically enjoy a reduced monthly rate compared to the monthly billing option. This presents an opportunity for bettors who are committed to using OddsJam over the long term to maximize savings and receive uninterrupted access to the platform's premium features throughout the year.

Savings and Cost-Effectiveness

Subscribers opting for annual billing not only benefit from lower monthly rates but also ensure cost-effectiveness in the long run. The annual billing option reflects a strategic decision for users confident in the platform's value and seeking a more economical approach to their subscription. The savings accrued over the course of a year can contribute to a more lucrative overall betting strategy.

Flexibility to Switch Plans

OddsJam often provides users with the flexibility to switch between plans based on their evolving needs. This ensures that users can adapt their subscription to match their changing betting preferences, whether they are exploring the platform, intensifying their betting strategies, or seeking different features offered by alternative plans.

OddsJam's Pricing and Savings structure caters to the diverse preferences and goals of sports bettors. The choice between monthly and annual billing options, coupled with potential savings for annual subscribers, ensures that users have the flexibility to tailor their subscription to align precisely with their betting strategies and commitment levels. Whether users prefer short-term flexibility or long-term savings, OddsJam's pricing options empower them to make informed decisions that suit their individual preferences and maximize their overall betting value.

Discounted Plans and Savings

OddsJam enhances its appeal to users by offering Discounted Plans and Savings, providing an avenue for subscribers to access premium features at a more affordable rate. This strategic approach aligns with OddsJam's commitment to making advanced sports betting tools accessible to a broader audience while still delivering substantial value.

Limited-Time Promotions

Periodically, OddsJam introduces limited-time promotions and discount plans, creating opportunities for users to capitalize on exclusive offers. These promotions may include reduced subscription fees, extended trial periods, or bundled packages, allowing users to access premium features at a discounted rate.

Seasonal Discounts

In the dynamic landscape of sports betting, OddsJam recognizes the influence of seasonal events and major sporting tournaments. To align with these occasions, the platform may introduce seasonal discounts, providing users with the chance to enjoy savings during specific periods, such as major sports seasons, championships, or sporting events.

Bundle Offers and Package Deals

OddsJam occasionally presents bundle offers and package deals, combining multiple premium features into a cost-effective package. Subscribers can benefit from a comprehensive suite of tools at a reduced overall cost, making it an attractive option for users seeking a bundled solution to enhance their sports betting strategies.

Loyalty and Referral Programs

As a gesture of appreciation to its user base, OddsJam may implement loyalty programs or referral incentives. Subscribers who remain committed to the platform over time or refer new users to OddsJam may be eligible for special discounts or additional savings, fostering a sense of community and rewarding user loyalty.

Limited-Time Trials for Premium Plans

OddsJam may introduce limited-time trials for its premium plans, allowing users to experience the full range of features at a discounted rate or even for free during the trial period. This gives users an opportunity to explore advanced tools, assess their effectiveness, and decide whether to continue with a discounted subscription.

Discounted Plans and Savings on OddsJam demonstrate the platform's commitment to making sophisticated sports betting tools accessible to a diverse user base. By introducing various promotional strategies, seasonal discounts, bundle offers, and loyalty programs, OddsJam ensures that users can access premium features at more affordable rates, empowering them to enhance their betting strategies while maximizing overall value. The availability of discounted plans adds an extra layer of versatility to OddsJam's subscription options, catering to users with varying preferences and budget considerations.

User Testimonials

User testimonials on OddsJam serve as a powerful testament to the platform's efficacy in transforming sports betting experiences. These testimonials, composed of user experiences and success stories, provide valuable insights into how OddsJam has played a pivotal role in enhancing the profitability, strategy, and overall satisfaction of individuals engaged in sports wagering.

Diverse Range of Success Stories

One of the standout features of OddsJam testimonials is the diversity of success stories shared by users. From novice bettors to seasoned professionals, individuals with varying levels of experience contribute their narratives, showcasing how OddsJam's tools have made a tangible impact on their betting journey. These success stories resonate with a broad audience, illustrating that OddsJam caters to users across the entire spectrum of sports betting expertise.

Improved Profitability and Returns

Numerous testimonials highlight how OddsJam's tools, particularly the Positive Expected Value (+EV) feature, have significantly improved users' profitability. Users express how leveraging OddsJam's data-driven insights has enabled them to identify bets with positive expected value, leading to more successful wagers and increased returns on investment. The platform's commitment to providing a mathematical edge is evident in these success stories, where users experience tangible financial gains.

Navigating Complex Strategies

Testimonials often delve into the complexity of sports betting strategies and how

OddsJam has simplified the process for users. From arbitrage betting to creating parlays with the Parlay Builder, users share how OddsJam's tools have made intricate strategies more accessible. The platform's educational resources, including tutorial videos and coaching sessions, contribute to users' ability to navigate and implement these strategies effectively.

Community Support and Interaction

User testimonials frequently touch upon the sense of community and support fostered by OddsJam. Users appreciate not only the platform's features but also the opportunity to connect with fellow bettors. Whether through forum discussions, shared insights, or collaborative learning experiences, the OddsJam community provides a supportive environment where users can exchange ideas and enhance their understanding of sports betting.

Platform Reliability and Real-Time Data

The reliability of OddsJam's platform and the real-time nature of its data receive acclaim in many testimonials. Users emphasize the importance of having accurate and up-to-date information when making betting decisions, and OddsJam consistently delivers on this front. Testimonials underscore how real-time push notifications, auto-refresh features, and live game odds contribute to users' confidence in their betting choices.

Transforming Casual Bettors into Informed Investors

Testimonials often recount the transformation of casual bettors into informed investors. Users share how OddsJam's tools have elevated their approach from casual gambling to strategic and calculated decision-making. The +EV

Tool, in particular, is lauded for its role in providing users with a deeper understanding of odds and probabilities, transforming their betting practices into more informed and strategic endeavors.

Educational Resources Making an Impact.

The impact of OddsJam's educational resources is a recurring theme in user testimonials. Users appreciate the tutorial videos, coaching sessions, and other learning materials that contribute to their growth as sports bettors. Many testimonials highlight how these resources have empowered users with knowledge, enabling them to make more informed decisions and ultimately succeed in their betting pursuits.

Navigating Challenges and Overcoming Skepticism

Some testimonials delve into the challenges users faced before discovering OddsJam and how the platform helped them overcome skepticism. Whether it's skepticism about the legitimacy of certain betting strategies or doubts about the effectiveness of sports betting tools, users express how OddsJam has provided them with clarity, guidance, and tangible results that dispel initial reservations.

Building Confidence and Overcoming Losses

Several testimonials explore the psychological aspect of sports betting, particularly how OddsJam has contributed to building confidence and overcoming losses. Users share how the platform's tools, educational resources, and community support have played a crucial role in helping them bounce back from setbacks, learn from mistakes, and approach betting with a more resilient and strategic mindset.

Loyalty and Long-Term Satisfaction.

A notable aspect of many testimonials is the loyalty and long-term satisfaction expressed by users. Individuals share how their positive experiences with OddsJam have led to continued subscription renewals, indicating a high level of satisfaction with the platform's ongoing value. This loyalty underscores the enduring impact of OddsJam on users' sports betting journeys.

The testimonials on OddsJam reflect a dynamic tapestry of user experiences and success stories. From financial gains and improved profitability to the transformation of betting approaches and the creation of a supportive community, these testimonials paint a vivid picture of the positive impact OddsJam has had on users across various aspects of sports betting. The platform's commitment to education, real-time data, community engagement, and user empowerment is evident in these narratives, making OddsJam not just a platform for tools but a catalyst for transformation and success in the dynamic and competitive world of sports wagering.

Frequently Asked Questions

How Does OddsJam Work?

OddsJam operates as a comprehensive sports betting platform that empowers users with advanced tools and data-driven insights to enhance their betting strategies. The platform's functionality can be summarized through the following key aspects:

Odds Comparison

At the core of OddsJam's functionality is its robust odds comparison feature. The platform aggregates and compares odds from various sportsbooks, providing users with a comprehensive view of the betting landscape. This empowers users to identify the most favorable odds for their preferred events and markets.

Positive Expected Value (+EV) Tool

OddsJam's +EV Tool is a centerpiece that calculates the expected value of bets based on statistical analysis. This tool helps users identify bets where the implied probability is lower than the calculated probability, indicating potential value. By focusing on +EV bets, users can make more informed and strategic wagering decisions.

Arbitrage Betting

The platform includes an Arbitrage feature that identifies opportunities for users to engage in arbitrage betting. This involves placing simultaneous bets on all possible outcomes of an event across different sportsbooks to secure a guaranteed profit. OddsJam streamlines this process, making arbitrage betting more accessible and efficient for users.

Educational Resources

OddsJam places a strong emphasis on user education. The platform provides tutorial videos, coaching sessions, and a wealth of educational resources to help users understand sports betting concepts, utilize platform tools effectively, and implement successful strategies. This commitment to education sets OddsJam apart as a comprehensive learning hub for both novice and experienced bettors.

Real-Time Updates

Real-time data is a crucial aspect of OddsJam's functionality. The platform continuously updates odds, ensuring users have the latest information to make timely decisions. Real-time push notifications and auto-refresh features contribute to a seamless user experience, allowing bettors to stay ahead of market changes.

Community Engagement

OddsJam fosters a sense of community among its users. Through forums, discussions, and community interactions, users can share insights, strategies, and experiences. This collaborative environment enhances the overall betting experience, providing users with a platform to learn from one another and stay informed about industry trends.

OddsJam works by combining cutting-edge technology, data analysis, and a commitment to user education to create a comprehensive platform for sports bettors. By offering a suite of tools, real-time updates, and a supportive community, OddsJam provides users with the resources and insights needed to navigate the complexities of sports betting and make informed, strategic decisions.

What are the Sportsbooks Requirements on OddsJam?

To fully leverage the powerful tools and features offered by OddsJam, users need to meet certain requirements related to the integration of sportsbooks and platform functionality. These requirements are designed to ensure a seamless and effective experience for users engaging with the OddsJam platform:

Sportsbook Accounts

Users must have active accounts with the sportsbooks integrated into the OddsJam platform. This involves creating accounts with reputable sports betting providers that OddsJam supports. These accounts serve as the foundation for users to execute bets and capitalize on identified opportunities.

Multiple Sportsbook Accounts

For optimal results, it is beneficial for users to have accounts with multiple sportsbooks. This allows OddsJam to compare odds across a diverse range of providers, maximizing the chances of identifying the most favorable betting opportunities. Having accounts with various sportsbooks enhances the flexibility and choice available to users.

Funding Sportsbook Accounts

To execute bets identified through OddsJam, users need to ensure their sportsbook accounts are adequately funded. This involves depositing funds into the accounts, providing the necessary capital to place wagers based on the platform's recommendations. The ability to fund accounts promptly is crucial for taking advantage of time-sensitive opportunities.

Platform Subscription

Users must subscribe to one of OddsJam's plans to access the premium features and tools offered by the platform. This subscription provides users with the full suite of tools, including the +EV Tool, Arbitrage, and other advanced features that enhance their sports betting strategies.

Technical Requirements

Users should have access to a reliable internet connection and a compatible device, such as a computer or mobile device, to effectively engage with OddsJam. This ensures a smooth and uninterrupted experience when navigating the platform, analyzing data, and placing bets.

Compliance with Sportsbook Rules

Users need to adhere to the rules and regulations set forth by the sportsbooks they are affiliated with. This includes complying with terms and conditions, responsible betting practices, and any specific requirements imposed by individual sportsbooks. Staying informed about sportsbook policies is essential for a positive and sustainable betting experience.

By meeting these sportsbooks requirements, users can unlock the full potential of OddsJam's tools and features. The integration of multiple sportsbooks, coupled with compliance with platform and sportsbook regulations, creates a symbiotic relationship where users can confidently implement strategic betting decisions based on real-time data and analysis provided by OddsJam.

What Time Commitment is required when using OddsJam?

The time commitment required to effectively utilize OddsJam depends on various factors, including individual preferences, betting strategies, and the level of engagement desired. Here's a breakdown of the key considerations regarding the time commitment when using OddsJam:

Flexibility for Casual Users

Casual users looking to explore sports betting as a form of entertainment can engage with OddsJam at their own pace. The platform caters to users with varying time availability, allowing them to access tools, compare odds, and place bets as leisure activities. Casual users can enjoy the flexibility to invest as much or as little time as they desire.

Strategic Planning for Intermediate Users.

Intermediate users who aim to enhance their betting strategies and capitalize on opportunities identified by OddsJam may choose to invest more time. This involves regular checks on the platform, staying informed about market changes, and strategically placing bets based on the recommendations provided. This level of engagement can lead to a more systematic and informed betting approach.

Professional-Level Commitment for Serious Bettors

Serious bettors, including those aiming for consistent profits and utilizing advanced features like arbitrage and +EV calculations, may commit more time to OddsJam. This involves continuous monitoring of odds, leveraging real-time updates, and actively participating in the community discussions. Serious bettors often view sports betting as a dedicated endeavor, and OddsJam becomes a comprehensive tool for their strategic decision-making.

Time-Sensitive Opportunities

The nature of sports betting includes time-sensitive opportunities, such as changes in odds or promotions with limited durations. Users seeking to capitalize on these opportunities may need to allocate specific time slots for active engagement with OddsJam, especially during peak betting periods or major sporting events.

Balancing Research and Execution

The time commitment also involves a balance between research and execution. Users may spend time analyzing data, watching tutorial videos, and participating in coaching sessions to enhance their understanding of betting strategies. Efficient execution of bets based on this research contributes to a well-rounded and time-effective approach.

The time commitment on OddsJam is highly adaptable to individual preferences and goals. Whether users are casual bettors enjoying occasional wagers, intermediate users refining their strategies, or serious bettors aiming for consistent profits, OddsJam accommodates a spectrum of time commitments. The platform's flexibility allows users to tailor their engagement based on their level of interest and desired outcomes in the dynamic world of sports betting.

What are the Winning Expectations on OddsJam?

Understanding winning expectations is a crucial aspect of utilizing OddsJam effectively. The platform provides users with powerful tools and data-driven insights to enhance their sports betting strategies, but it's essential for users to approach their expectations realistically and in line with the dynamic nature of sports wagering:

Positive Expected Value (+EV) Strategy

The +EV strategy employed by OddsJam revolves around identifying bets with positive expected value, where the implied probability is lower than the calculated probability. While this approach provides a mathematical edge, users should recognize that positive expected value does not guarantee immediate or consistent wins. It is a strategic approach that, over time, increases the likelihood of profitable outcomes.

Arbitrage Opportunities

Arbitrage betting, another feature of OddsJam, involves placing simultaneous bets on all possible outcomes of an event across different sportsbooks to secure a guaranteed profit. Users need to approach arbitrage with a realistic understanding of potential returns and the need for swift execution, as these opportunities are often time-sensitive.

Varied Betting Outcomes

Sports betting inherently involves an element of unpredictability. Users should acknowledge that even with OddsJam's tools and insights, outcomes can vary. Factors such as unexpected player performance, injuries, or other unforeseen events can influence results. Realistic expectations involve recognizing that no strategy can eliminate all elements of risk.

Consistency and Long-Term Perspective

OddsJam encourages a consistent and long-term perspective towards sports betting. While individual bets may result in losses, the overall strategy should be geared towards achieving profitability over an extended period. Consistency in applying informed decision-making and utilizing OddsJam's features contributes to sustainable success.

Bankroll Management

Managing one's bankroll is crucial in aligning winning expectations with a sustainable betting approach. Users should set realistic and achievable goals, considering their financial capacity. Effective bankroll management, combined with strategic betting decisions, contributes to a balanced and responsible approach to sports wagering.

Continuous Learning and Adaptation

Winning expectations are also tied to a user's commitment to continuous learning and adaptation. The sports betting landscape evolves, and OddsJam provides educational resources, tutorial videos, and coaching sessions to help users refine their strategies and stay ahead of industry trends. A willingness to adapt based on insights gained contributes to improved winning expectations.

Winning expectations on OddsJam should be approached with a balanced perspective that recognizes the inherent uncertainties in sports betting. While the platform equips users with valuable tools and strategies, success is best measured over the long term, with an understanding that individual outcomes may vary. Realistic expectations, coupled with a commitment to continuous learning and strategic decision-making, contribute to a positive and sustainable sports betting experience with OddsJam.

How does OddsJam Address Scam Concerns?

Addressing scam concerns is a valid consideration in the realm of online platforms, especially those related to finance and betting. However, OddsJam prioritizes transparency, user trust, and compliance with industry standards to alleviate any apprehensions related to potential scams:

Transparency and Reputation

OddsJam maintains a transparent and reputable presence in the sports betting community. The platform has garnered positive reviews and testimonials from users who have experienced success with its tools. Transparency in displaying odds, features, and subscription plans contributes to establishing trust among users.

Legitimate Business Operations

OddsJam operates as a legitimate business entity, complying with relevant laws and regulations. Users can verify the platform's credentials, including licensing information, to ensure that it adheres to industry standards. Legitimate operations and adherence to regulatory requirements contribute to user confidence in the platform.

Trial Period and Money-Back Guarantee

To address concerns and allow users to experience the platform's capabilities risk-free, OddsJam offers a trial period for its subscription plans. Additionally, the platform often provides a money-back guarantee, allowing users to request a refund within a specified period if they are dissatisfied with the services. These features demonstrate OddsJam's commitment to user satisfaction.

User Support and Communication

OddsJam maintains open lines of communication with its user base. The platform offers responsive customer support to address queries and concerns promptly. Clear communication channels contribute to building trust and assuring users that their questions or issues will be addressed in a timely manner.

Educational Resources and Community Engagement

OddsJam distinguishes itself by providing extensive educational resources and fostering community engagement. These efforts go beyond typical scam practices, emphasizing the platform's commitment to user empowerment and education. The availability of tutorial videos, coaching sessions, and community forums reinforces OddsJam's dedication to user support.

Secure Transactions and Data Protection

OddsJam prioritizes the security of user transactions and personal information. The platform employs encryption measures to safeguard user data and financial transactions. This commitment to data protection ensures that users can engage with the platform confidently, knowing that their information is handled securely.

Positive User Experiences

Positive user experiences, as reflected in testimonials, serve as a testament to OddsJam's legitimacy and effectiveness. Users who have successfully utilized the platform's tools share their stories, contributing to a positive reputation and dispelling concerns related to potential scams.

OddsJam addresses scam concerns through a combination of transparency, legitimate business practices, user support, and a commitment to user education. The platform's focus on building a trustworthy reputation, coupled with features like trial periods and money-back guarantees, contributes to user confidence and reinforces OddsJam's position as a reliable and reputable platform in the sports betting landscape.

How can I Balance Effort and Rewards on OddsJam?

Achieving a harmonious balance between the effort invested and the rewards reaped is pivotal for users navigating the dynamic landscape of sports betting through OddsJam. Striking this equilibrium involves a thoughtful approach, considering individual preferences, goals, and the multifaceted nature of sports wagering:

Customizable Strategies

OddsJam recognizes that users have varying levels of time and effort they can commit to sports betting. The platform's tools and features are designed to accommodate customizable strategies, allowing users to tailor their approach based on the effort they are willing to invest and the rewards they seek.

Casual Betting Enjoyment

For users seeking casual enjoyment from sports betting, OddsJam offers a user-friendly interface and straightforward tools. Casual bettors can engage with the platform at their own pace, enjoying occasional bets without requiring an extensive time commitment. The platform's flexibility ensures that even with minimal effort, users can find value and entertainment.

Strategic Decision-Making for Intermediate Users

Intermediate users looking to enhance their betting strategies may choose to allocate more effort to OddsJam. This involves deeper engagement with educational resources, regular checks on odds, and a strategic approach to placing bets. The platform empowers intermediate users to make informed decisions, balancing effort with the potential rewards.

Dedication for Serious Bettors

Serious bettors aiming for consistent profits often choose to dedicate more time and effort to OddsJam. Engaging with advanced features, such as arbitrage and +EV calculations, requires a commitment to continuous monitoring and swift decision-making. Serious bettors view sports betting as an endeavor that merits a more significant investment of time and strategic effort.

Sustainable Long-Term Perspective

Balancing effort and rewards involves adopting a sustainable long-term perspective. Users are encouraged to view sports betting as an ongoing journey rather than seeking immediate gains. Consistent effort, coupled with disciplined bankroll management and strategic decision-making, contributes to sustainable success over time.

Risk Management

Effectively balancing effort and rewards also involves prudent risk management. Users should assess the level of risk they are comfortable with and align their betting strategies accordingly. OddsJam provides tools and insights to assist users in making risk-informed decisions, contributing to a balanced and well-managed approach.

OddsJam caters to users with diverse preferences by offering a platform that accommodates various levels of effort and commitment. Whether users are seeking casual enjoyment, refining their strategies, or pursuing sports betting as a serious endeavor, OddsJam provides the tools and resources to strike a meaningful balance between effort and rewards. The platform's versatility empowers users to engage in sports betting on their terms, fostering an environment where individuals can find fulfillment and success based on their unique goals and levels of commitment.

What is the Cancellation Process on OddsJam?

OddsJam understands that user needs and preferences may evolve over time, and as such, provides a straightforward and user-friendly cancellation process for those who may wish to discontinue their subscription. Here's an overview of the cancellation process on OddsJam:

User Account Access

To initiate the cancellation process, users need to access their OddsJam account. This typically involves logging in with their credentials on the platform's website.

Subscription Management Section

Within the user account interface, there is a dedicated Subscription Management section. This section is designed to provide users with clear and accessible options related to their subscription, including cancellation.

Cancellation Request

Users wishing to cancel their subscription can navigate to the designated cancellation request page within the Subscription Management section. Here, they may find a straightforward form or a series of steps to follow, guiding them through the cancellation process.

Confirmation and Verification

Once the cancellation request is submitted, OddsJam may require users to confirm their decision. This confirmation step ensures that the cancellation is intentional and helps prevent accidental cancellations.

Communication and Support

OddsJam values user feedback and is likely to facilitate communication during the cancellation process. This may include providing users with information about the next steps, confirming the cancellation request, and addressing any questions or concerns users may have.

Refund Policy (if applicable)

Depending on the specific circumstances and the terms of service, OddsJam may have a refund policy in place. Users should review this policy to understand if they are eligible for a refund based on the timing of their cancellation and the platform's terms.

Immediate or Scheduled Cancellation

The cancellation process on OddsJam may lead to immediate termination of premium features or may be scheduled to take effect at the end of the current billing cycle, depending on the platform's policies. This allows users to continue accessing their subscription benefits until the end of the prepaid period.

OddsJam aims to make the cancellation process as transparent and user-friendly as possible, respecting the choices of users and ensuring a hassle-free experience. By providing clear steps, communication, and potential refund options, the platform prioritizes user satisfaction even in the event of subscription cancellation.

Conclusion

Customer Support

OddsJam recognizes the importance of effective customer support to enhance user experiences and address any queries or concerns that may arise. The platform provides multiple avenues for users to reach out and seek assistance through its dedicated customer support services:

Email Support

Users can utilize the email support option to communicate directly with OddsJam's customer support team. This method allows for detailed explanations of issues or inquiries, and users can expect a timely response to their emails. The email support address is typically provided on the OddsJam website or within the user account interface.

Live Chat

OddsJam often offers a live chat feature for real-time assistance. Users can engage in instant messaging with a customer support representative, making it convenient for addressing urgent matters or seeking quick clarifications. Live chat enhances the accessibility of support, providing users with immediate responses to their queries.

Help Center Resources

OddsJam maintains a comprehensive Help Center with informative articles, frequently asked questions, and guides that cover various aspects of the platform. Users can explore this resource to find answers to common queries without directly reaching out to customer support.

Community Forums

The OddsJam community forums also serve as a valuable resource for users seeking assistance. While not a direct customer support channel, the forums enable users to engage with the community, share experiences, and potentially find solutions to common issues by learning from the experiences of fellow users.

Social Media Channels

OddsJam may utilize social media channels to communicate with users and address inquiries. Users can follow OddsJam on platforms like Twitter or Facebook to stay updated on announcements, receive support-related information, and potentially reach out to the customer support team through these channels.

Response Time Commitment

OddsJam is committed to providing timely responses to user inquiries. The platform typically outlines its response time commitments, ensuring that users can expect a prompt and efficient resolution to their concerns.

OddsJam's customer support is designed to be accessible and responsive, offering users multiple channels to seek assistance. Whether through email, live chat, the Help

Center, community forums, or social media, OddsJam aims to foster open communication and address user needs effectively. The customer support team plays a crucial role in ensuring that users have a positive and supportive experience while navigating the platform's features and maximizing their sports betting strategies.

Dear Reader,

I hope you enjoyed reading this book! Your feedback is incredibly valuable to me, and I would love to hear your thoughts. If you found the book insightful, entertaining, or if there's anything specific you appreciated, please consider leaving a review.

Your reviews not only provide valuable insights for future readers but also motivate and support authors like myself. Whether it's a brief comment or a detailed review, your opinion matters.

Thank you for taking the time to share your thoughts. I appreciate your support and hope the book left a positive impact on your reading journey.

Happy reading!

Best regards,
Paul N Roy

Printed in Great Britain
by Amazon